A LETTER
TO
RUDRAPUR

SAMEER THE GREAT

ISBN 979-888569837-5

"Gururbrahma gururvishnuh gururdevo maheshwarah,

Gurursakshat Parabrahma Tasmai Sri Gurve Namah.

Meaning:- Guru is like Brahma (the creator). Guru is like Vishnu (protector). Guru Prabhu is like Maheshwar (destroyer). The True Guru is the Supreme Brahma (God) before the eyes. I bow to my true Guru."

I am striving to know the truth of life, therefore I am an obedient and guru bhakt student. There is nothing in my life more than a Guru. I consider all the material and non-material elements of this world as my Guru. I do most of my work with discipline, as I don't want to repeat any mistake. Often the same person makes a mistake, who lives in an imaginary world beyond the truth.

Since my God-like guru Dr. Pragyan Choudhary has associated me with Sri Aurobindo Society, the entire credit for every positive change in my life in this context goes to my guru. Apart from this, Swami Brahmdev ji, a guru equivalent in writing this letter, Shri Anna ji for inciting me and all the participants of the camp for being an accomplice, deserve to be congratulated for this noble work. I am publishing my letter in front of you through this small booklet so that you can understand the past and present and avoid possible mistakes in future. By the way, some people have deviated from the right path, because some clever people are playing with the sentiments of the common people and diverting them. My aim is that I can do the work of showing people the right path. I am also successful in this endeavor. As long as I live, I will keep trying endlessly. Being grateful to Pragyan sir, Shokendra sir and my parents, I dedicate all my successes to them. In the end I dedicate a verse to all my true Gurus:-

"*Tvameva mata Cha pita Tvameva, Tvameva bandhoosch Cha Sakha Tvameva, Tvameva Vidya Cha Dravinam Tvameva, Tvameva Sarvam Mam Devdevam.*

Meaning:- '*Oh my God! You are the mother, you are the father, you are the brother, you are the friend. You are knowledge, you are material, you are everything. You are my God.*'"

Date:- 25/01/2022

Sameer The Great

Contents

Preface

At present, this world is struggling with all kinds of new problems, but India is struggling with some old problems along with new ones. Among the old problems, caste system, sometimes religious hysteria, sometimes malpractices and hypocrisy etc. are prominent. Surprisingly, some people do not want to let the situation normalize in India. It is our utmost duty to refute such selfish people. Only when we work in the right direction can our country be saved. Therefore, you should extend your hand in the discharge of the high conscious human duties inaugurated by Maharishi Aurobindo. After this humanitarian work, you can save the nation as well as the whole world.

Date:- 25/01/2022

Sameer The Great.

Prologue

I have given most of the information in the previous chapters. Now I don't want to delay any longer. Through this small book and letter, I want to give a signal to the dear people of humanity, that all of you should rise above caste, religion and sect and move forward on the path of becoming a higher human being supported by Sri Aurobindo. By this work you will contribute to the salvation of the whole world.

Date:- 25/01/2022

Sameer The Great.

Acknowledgements

"Jeena Tabhi Seekhte Hai,
Jab Koi Na Ho Sahara,
Dhanyavad Un Logo Ko,
Jinhone Chhoda Hume Besahara."

Foreword

Who is greater than the creator? In this mortal world, man has become so mad after material comforts, that he himself has become the destroyer of nature. Even after spending lakhs and crores of rupees, when a person is not satisfied, then he is able to take a breath of peace only by going to the lap of nature at the last moment. Today's man pretends to cry before the imaginary God, and ignores the true God. Why does such a situation arise? Does the person not know the truth or is he deliberately repeating the mistake? You may also be thinking that what is the reality after all? In fact, man has gone astray at present, because many people and organizations are working with a specific goal to make him go astray. Knowingly or unknowingly some common people are also bringing their ruin closer by giving unnecessary benefits to those organizations. Who is at a loss in this emotion game? Maybe you guys would not know that humanity is going to end in this game. In the coming times, the word humanity will look good only in books, because human beings have crossed all the limits of being called human. Modern man has only a selfish and hollow physical body left. But from time to time some divine men have appeared on this earth to awaken the people, because when the problems in the society increase more, then some people take their step forward to find their solution. They eradicate that problem after sacrificing their whole life.

"Yada yada hi Dharmasya glanirbhavati Bharat,
abhyutthanam dharmasya tadatmanam
srijamayam.
Paritranaya Sadhunam Vinashaya Cha

Duskritam,
Dharmsansthapnarthay Sambhavami Yuge
Yuge.
Meaning- I appear, I come, when there is loss of
righteousness, then I come, when unrighteousness
increases then I come, to protect the gentlemen, I
come to destroy the wicked. I come for this, I come
for the establishment of religion and take birth in
the age of age. "

In this sequence, Maharishi Aurobindo Ghosh, a great scholar born in the 19th century, had worked tirelessly to awaken the sleeping consciousness of the people of the then India. At the end of their attempt, they were also successful. He passed the ICS examination after getting education in England and deliberately failed in it. Later he worked in a princely state called Gujarat located in India. He tried to remove the mental disorders of most of the people of India. Arvind was such a serious person, that the British used to fear him. There came a time when the publication of books, magazines and magazines written by him were also banned. But some people are very stubborn, those who are determined, they do it. Arvind Ghosh was also one of those stubborn people. The clouds of untruth could not stand in front of the storm of truth in the form of their stubbornness.

It is not a book, it is a letter. I wrote this on 27th December 2021 after the conclusion of Auro Youth Camp. After writing this letter, I sent it to the Rudrapur branch of Sri Aurobindo Society. I do not know how important this letter is. But I know that this is no ordinary letter. I don't want to say much more about this. I just want to say that this letter will reveal the secrets of past to present and future. After reading this you will understand for yourself.

By the way, I have mentioned this letter in my first book **Aurovalley The Secrets of My Journey**. If you want to know the relevance of this letter in more depth, then you can also read the above book. Now without delay, I am presenting the 11 page letter written by me to you guys:-

My Book:- Aurovalley The Secrets of My Journey

CHAPTER I

1st Page of Letter

To The,
Rudrapur Branch,
Shri Aurobindo Society,
Udham Singh Nagar, Uttarakhand,
India.
Pin code - 263153.

I would consider it appropriate to surrender my full consciousness to every enlightened being who walks impartially on the path guided by Sri Aurobindo and Sri Maa. I bow before all those divine souls who are trying objectively with true devotion and dedication to attain the higher humanity as directed by Sri Aurobindo.

Perhaps our memories form our history, and our history itself gives us the identity of our civilization and culture. In fact, the land of India has been full of divine talents leading one of the world's oldest advanced civilizations and cultures. From the Vedic age to the modern technological age, there have been many such great men in India, who have worked tirelessly to show the eternal path to the society of the world including India. The Vedas are mentioned in the oldest texts of the world, the Vedas were also composed in India. After this Gautam Buddha gave such a unique philosophy to the world that many countries of the world are moving towards success by following him till date. Mahavir Swami also happened during this period. Like Buddha, he gave the message of complete non-violence to the world by becoming a saint, sacrificing the material comforts of the world and living separately from the people. Then gradually, many religious or spiritual leaders took the policy leadership of all the regional dynasties. Many texts were composed under the guidance of these gurus. In which Chanakya's Arthashastra is a major book. Gradually, in the medieval period, Saint Raidas, Kabir, Guru Nanak and Sufi saints guided and guided the policy of the then dynasties with their philosophy and criticism.

CHAPTER II

2nd Page of Letter

Later some intelligent people probably introduced the idea of religion and God to keep people united. Most of the people settled in different regions of the world considered it appropriate to worship the budding religion and God of their particular region. All budding religions had a single objective, to strengthen the internal security of their state (territorial unit) while keeping the people united. Different countries of each continent often used to fight on the basis of one religion, so that the unity of the people living in that particular region is not fragmented. The unity of the people of a particular region opened the way for the emergence of new nations in the future, the newly created nations were mainly inspired by race or religion etc. But gradually the deteriorating nature of religion played an important role in fragmenting the human unity of the world. In the colonial period, the blind race of selfishness of the imperialist people became the reason for the exploitation of all the innocent people. At that time, the industrialization of western countries had changed the society and culture of most of the world. The whole world had become a mere market for imports and exports. The imperialist countries started exploiting their colonial territory with economic, human, environmental and cultural intensity and tried to achieve the inhuman aspiration to improve their nation by destroying other nations. The condition of the common people of Indian society deteriorated in the blind race of industrial and colonial exchange, it had a negative effect on the mentality of the Indian people. Since, as in the present, most of the people used to indulge in material comforts and facilities, so they, being ignorant of reality, continued to suffer their slavery and exploitation as the result of rebirth. But some people, understanding the pain and pain of this slavery and exploitation, opposed them to get rid of them. In this episode some liberals and some extremists strongly opposed the colonial forces in their own way. After that, along with some revolutionaries, the Father of the Nation, Mahatma Gandhi also sacrificed his whole life to get freedom for India. After independence, the 'recovery of the lost honor of most people and women of India' was a big challenge before the then leaders. Some specific people took the initiative to find a solution to this problem. After this, Dr. BR Ambedkar assisted the Constituent Assembly in creating the world's largest written constitution.

CHAPTER III

3rd Page of Letter

In the newly made constitution, arrangements were made to provide social, economic and political justice to all the people of India. Following the footsteps of this constitution, today India is setting new records of development.

In the last decade of the 19th century, a young man who had returned from England after studying had understood that in order to awaken the sleeping people of India, the consciousness of the Indian people would have to be awakened and to awaken their consciousness, they would have to explain the ultimate truth. And to understand the ultimate truth, they have to give holistic education. To achieve these objectives and principles, that young man sacrificed his life to awaken innocent people. After suffering a lot in his life, he had to make Pondicherry his new home and there he devoted his entire life to the cause of humanity. This great man will later be called Shri Arvind, I salute him from the bottom of my heart.

Just as Karl Marx and Engels are mentioned together, similarly Sri Aurobindo and Sri Maa are also mentioned together, because like Marx and Engels Sri Aurobindo and Sri Maa are inseparably linked and these The pure knowledge gained from this association of great men has dazzled the world till date.

Parents play a big role in the full development of every child, because they can give good environment and good values to the child. The responsibility of early education also rests to a great extent on the parents. If the parents themselves are not educated, then the chances of children getting spoiled are also high. The entire society and humanity has to bear the brunt of the deterioration of any child. But we should not give full blame to parents, as they are bound in worldly responsibilities. After discharging their responsibilities, they would not be able to give much time to the children in the remaining time. But there is nothing to panic because the solution to this problem is present in the system.

CHAPTER IV

4th Page of Letter

There is a guru in the form of God (from primary education to higher education) to eradicate this problem of theirs, provided the parents themselves take the trouble of taking the children to the guru. Undoubtedly a true Guru makes every effort to make each of his disciples a true and good human being, provided the disciple is also ready to become a good human being with complete devotion to his True Guru.

My life has also been the same as the life of ordinary people. In my life, apart from my parents, time has played an important role in becoming my teacher and I have learned a lot by considering time as a teacher. After that, from my childhood, I continue to meet all the true and good gurus (physical or non-material), with whose cooperation and blessings I continued to grow. But my endless search was still on, because I could not find what I was looking for, i.e. the one who could give peace to my soul (exploratory mind), who could give me inner satisfaction (answers to esoteric questions) (my brain) I used to have many questions, I was looking for a good teacher to know the answer to those questions). I hoped that they would meet me and I kept on trying endlessly, finally my efforts worked and I was successful. When I took admission in M.A. History of Digambar Jain Degree College, Baraut, Baghpat in the month of July 2017, then I met my God-formed Guru Dr. Pragyan Chaudhary and Dr. Shokendra Kumar Sharma. Pragyan sir was a true human being as well as a well-versed in the transcendental philosophy given by Shri Aurobindo and Shri Maa. He was an outstanding human being as well as a historian, philosopher, sociologist, psychologist, archaeologist, anthropologist, spiritual scholar, environmentalist, social worker, enlightened being, film director, an experienced person in the corporate and non-corporate sectors. . Many times I had seen that Pragyan sir, like Sri Aurobindo, did not take the credit for the work itself after completing it. Sir also had considerable interest in the spiritual realm, as a result it was a common practice to keep some spiritual and philosophical books on his table. Once at Sir's table (History Department, Digambar Jain Degree College Baraut, Baghpat) I saw the June edition of 2019's Agnishikha. I was sitting alone in the history department, so I picked it up from the head's table and started reading (I know it was my fault, because I shouldn't have touched anything without permission. But it's always my desire to learn something new.) Anxiety had broken my moral discipline). As soon as Sir came, I kept that book in its place and told Sir that this book is very good. After being quiet for a while, Sir replied politely, do you want this book? I naively bowed my neck down. Then sir gave me the book 'The Mother' along with 'Agnishikha'.

CHAPTER V

5th Page of Letter

He probably gave me the book 'The Mother' to read only after seeing my interests and aspirations. I started reading that book but it was somewhat incomprehensible (seems normal now). It was during this time that I also started reading a monthly magazine called Agnisika. I started taking interest in it and whenever I got time, I would read Agnishikha. Due to this, I got many benefits, one, the art of distinguishing between many evils and bad thoughts prevailing in the society was improved, secondly, my grip on Hindi language became better because most of the sentences printed in Agnisikha were full of serious Hindi words. A few months after this, in 2019 itself, Auro Youth Camp was to be organized by Sri Aurobindo Society, Sir, I had informed about it long before the event. But at that time I was on educational stay in Hapur, so could not attend the camp. I regretted it a lot. But my guru was aware and worried about this and he followed his guru dharma very well and gave me a sudden information about the organization of Auro Youth Camp of the year 2021 on the phone at around 9:00 PM on 21st December. To my surprise, my current condition wanted me to stop from any travel and tourism, yet I immediately said yes to go. My Guru automatically solved that invisible problem of mine too. He asked me to go to the camp (Raiwala, Dehradun) free from every worry. This was to be my first journey beyond Haridwar towards North India. I happily took a direct bus from Meerut to Rishikesh on 24th December 2021 from Dr. Bhimrao Ambedkar Hostel of Chaudhary

Charan Singh University, Meerut in the afternoon and got down Raiwala and reached Aurovali Ashram via e-rickshaw. I even fell asleep during the long bus journey. Meanwhile, calls from Kirti Sarkar ma'am and Vijay Kumar ji were getting repeated on my phone. I informed them to be on the bus and they helped me guide me. It was almost 5:00 PM to reach the ashram. I was a little late on time. That's why I had to apologize in front of Kirti Sarkar ji, because after waiting for my long, they started the activities of the camp. By the way, Pragyan sir told me to come before 3:00 PM and Kirti Sarkar ji told me to come by 1:00 PM. But it was my fault that I was late and I chose the wrong bus, because that bus stopped for a long time at many places, due to which I was very late.

CHAPTER VI

6th Page of Letter

On the evening of 24 December 2021, we were given some instructions and a poem was recited collectively, which was as follows:-

"**"Bird's Nest"**
First of all my house was shaped like an egg,
Then I used to understand that the world is like this
only.
Then my home made nest made of dry straws,
Even then, she used to understand that the world is
just like that.
Then I left
Even then she used to understand that the world is
like this.
But when I flew in the sky, my wings spread far and
wide,
Only then did I understand that this world is very
big.
This world is very big..... "

Through this poem, we were told that till we do not leave the house, we consider our house and the things around us as the world, but when we go out to see the world, then we understand It turns out that in reality the world is very strange and vast. Then at 6:00 in the evening, we went to the meditation hall for meditation and there all the companions did meditation sitting in the posture of meditation. After that we came to the Vishwa Mandir and after resting for an hour, at 8:00 PM, all the companions reached their respective rooms to sleep after having dinner. The next day from 6:00 AM to 9:00 PM the program list was ready and starting with yoga and exercise in the morning, we ended our first day of Christmas celebration. Similarly, on 26th also we participated in many types of competitions and tried to recognize our inner strength. In this endeavor we were trying to awaken the indomitable aspiration to develop our consciousness. But due to different age and experience of all the participants in the limited time, it was not possible to achieve this desired goal by all. If each partner makes a sincere effort, he can be successful by taking himself on the long journey of making himself super human. Before lighting the lamp on 26th December Shri Anna ji sang the following song with us:-

CHAPTER VII

7th Page of Letter

*"**"The Choice of Eternal Truth"***
One is ours and one is in their country, give voices,
Now it's up to you which voice you listen to what
you believe..!
We say that identification of insa by caste religion
is wrong,
They say that all humans are one, this declaration
is wrong.
We say that the decree of hatred is wrong.
They say that as if the whole of India is wrong.
We say that by mistake, talk about hate, love,
They say if there is bloodshed, let it happen.
One is ours and one is in their country, give voices,
Now it's up to you, which voice do you listen to
what you believe..!
We say that humans should love humans,
They say that the trident in the hands should be the
sword.
We say settle homeless homeless people,
They say: Remember the forgotten temple and
mosque.
One is ours and one is in their country, give voices,
Now it's up to you which voice you listen to what
you believe."

In fact, this song was very cryptic and considering it as
a whole person/society/country take the upcoming

decisions of their life, then perhaps the purpose of Sri Aurobindo and Sri Maa can be fulfilled, its importance is currently being considered by some people. Only the society/country will be able to understand that because bitter gourd vegetable is bitter, only few people like it. If the importance of this song is not understood and adopted at the moment, then it will take almost several centuries for India to return to its own Ayurveda, in the same way after several hundred years this song will be remembered again.

CHAPTER VIII

8th Page of Letter

On the last day of the 27th morning, we had to do shramdaan in the camp in the morning and leave for Haridwar after breakfast. In Haridwar some comrades took bath at Birla Ghat, some comrades also did shopping (I also bought a bag). After that till noon, first the Mathura group, then the Rudrapur group and then the Mohammadpur group walked towards the bus stand to go to their respective homes. I was also going along with the comrades of Mohammadpur group on the way on foot. Although I had to go with the friends of Rudrapur, but they did not go on foot and went by rickshaw, so I thought it appropriate to go with the people of Mohammadpur group. While leaving I was so engrossed in talking with them that I was proceeding on the same path with the Mohammadpur group, then one of them reminded me that your way is another, then I returned in surprise went on his way. After reaching the bus stand, I took a bus from Haridwar to Meerut and the bus dropped me at Sohrab Gate bus stand in Meerut around 6:00 PM from where I reached my hostel after catching an e-rickshaw.

The above description was only travelogue and memoir. In this description, I have made a macro presentation of my experience and events, but if I do a micro presentation, then some more serious truth can come out. Actually the purpose of the city of Auroville, established in Pondicherry by Sri Aurobindo and Sri Maa, was to develop the consciousness of the innocent human. But it can be very difficult for a human being to reach the ultimate truth established by Sri Aurobindo as soon as he deviates from this purpose. Actually we are living in such a time of the world where different countries, different races, different castes, different religions, different languages, different cultures, different food habits and There are different costumes etc. The root cause of this is the difference in social, economic, political, religious, cultural, historical and geographical conditions of the people. Because of these differences, establishing unity among all people is a very difficult task. Since ancient times, the caste system in Indian society has become a huge crisis in front of the social unity of India. Perhaps some human beings played an immoral game with religion out of greed for the supply of their material pleasures and some such selfish trick was played by which many such malpractices were born in the society, these malpractices were enough to create a rift in the society. Sri Aurobindo understood and studied all these problems and rising above caste, religion and nationalities, he established such a philosophy of divine love and equality which teaches to be bound in divine unity of all human beings of the earth. These principles present spiritual knowledge by developing the consciousness of man and making him super human from ordinary human beings.

CHAPTER IX

9th Page of Letter

In fact, spirituality is and should be quite different from religion (but some people are cleverly engaged in trying to identify spirituality and religion) because from ancient times to modern times we have learned through religion from the historical experience of mankind. One can see many serious problems created directly or indirectly. Long wars were fought for many years keeping religion or God at the center and millions of innocent people of the world were put to death in these wars. Even today, many such fundamentalist organizations and people keep doing such abominable work directly or indirectly. But the aim of Sri Aurobindo and Sri Maa was to show the right path to all their innocent children, so that their children do not repeat any mistake and try to become an excellent human by using their intelligence beyond a normal human. God had made us fully conscious, but the wall of selfishness and greed in between became so big that instead of going towards excellence, we moved towards inferiority. But now things are changing and slowly people are waking up and from dormant state man is moving towards complete light by erasing complete darkness in the conscious race of awakened state.

I met many new friends at camp. Some were younger, some were even older, some were boys and some were girls. Most of the companions were very good, some were very naughty, some were also very ignorant. Some of the companions were also victims of the misleading and frustrated truth of this unconscious society, while some were ignorant of all the customs and traditions of this world. Still, it was a matter of happiness that all the comrades were present on a platform which could give them the inspiration and opportunity to become a better and better person. Perhaps the dream of Shri Aurobindo and Shri Maa will be fulfilled on the day when we all understand the spiritual purpose of Shri Aurobindo very closely and take it literally in our lives. Sri Aurobindo does not mention, criticize or endorse any religion or caste. That is why conscious people who go towards the absolute truth as told by Sri Aurobindo and Sri Maa, should keep in mind that we follow all the rules properly, because even a small mistake spoils the system.

CHAPTER X

10th Page of Letter

मेरे गुरू एवं प्रोफेसर

Dr. Pragyan Choudhary
[M.A., M.Phil, Ph.D., UGC JRF]

Associate Professor,
(Head of Department)
Department of History,
Digambar Jain (P.G.) College,
Baraut, Baghpat,
Uttar Pradesh,
India.
Pin Code – 250611.

Chaudhary Charan Singh University,
Meerut, Uttar Pradesh, India.
Pin Code – 250004.

Dr. Shokendra Kumar Sharma
[M.A. (Gold Medalist), M.Phil, Ph.D, UGC NET]

Assistant Professor,
Department of History,
Digambar Jain (P.G.) College,
Baraut, Baghpat,
Uttar Pradesh,
India.
Pin Code – 250611.

Chaudhary Charan Singh University,
Meerut, Uttar Pradesh, India.
Pin Code – 250004.

10th Page of Letter

11th Page of Letter

11th Page of Letter

Sri Aurobindo Ghosh

Sri Aurobindo Ghosh